# EDIBLE ?
# INCREDIBLE!

Text, Photographs and Scientific Material
by
Marjorie Furlong and Virginia Pill

Seventh Edition, Revised March 1989

Printing by
Andover Printing
Seattle, Washington

ISBN 0-9616021-1-2

# ABOUT THE AUTHORS

*Virginia Pill* (left) is a long-time resident of beautiful Hood Canal, on Washington's Olympic Peninsula. She is an avid naturalist, and has traveled Western Washington's beaches and forests for many years seeking nature's bounty. Recently retired from the public school system, she and husband John have presented many demonstrations on marine life.

*Marjorie Furlong* (right) grew up in Western Washington. Foraging on the beaches of Puget Sound and the Pacific Ocean has been a way of life. For many years, she and husband Ed operated a sealife museum and aquarium on Hood Canal. She has traveled as far as Australia and the South Pacific collecting information and specimens. She has a great love and respect for all of nature which is reflected in this book.

# TABLE OF CONTENTS

# INTRODUCTION

Almost all sea life *is* EDIBLE! INCREDIBLE but true! Even the skeptics agree after tasting some of the unusual sea life in this book. This is not just another recipe book but a guide to help our readers utilize sea life that is often overlooked, wasted or needlessly destroyed.

We all need to learn about our sea shores in order to successfully preserve them for the future. In many regions, the ocean and its inhabitants have managed to survive the pollution and other changes caused by the earth's population explosion. It can continue to be a vast, worldwide supermarket with its harvest of abundant sea life, only through the individual's knowledge and concern for that life.

Properly controlled and farmed, the sea could produce a balanced diet for everyone. Sea plants are rich in minerals, traces of iodine, manganese, aluminum and a long list of other elements. Kelp seaweed may unknowingly already be part of your regular diet. Algin derived from kelp is used as a stabilizer or smoothing agent in puddings, ice cream, chocolate milk and whipped toppings, to mention a few. Toothpaste and shaving creams are some of the beauty aids that probably contain a derivative of kelp. Carrageen gel, produced from a red seaweed, has proven useful for skin care because of its smoothing, healing and firming properties. Sea farming in many countries is an important industry. Unfortunately, only a small fraction of our vast coastline has supervised farming at the present time. Our hope is that this book will stimulate interest and familiarize the reader with what can be harvested from the beach.

Although we have illustrated and described sea life primarily found in West Coast waters, the recipes and preparation instructions for eating are generally applicable to similar life found worldwide. Most of this marine life can be found intertidally, between high and extremely low tides. The deeper water forms, such as octopus, squid and sea cucumber, are often inadvertently caught by hook and line while fishing or brought up with a shrimp, crab or lobster pot. For instance, if you catch an octopus or squid, don't be squeamish and throw it back, for it is delicious when properly prepared. Octopus and squid are harmless creatures and not the fearsome demons of fiction stories.

To aid in identification, the reader will find at least one color illustration and description for each suggested edible sea life.

For the beach forager, we have given likely areas where to look for each animal or plant, and ways to clean and prepare this saltwater delight. After sea life is gathered, it is best when prepared and eaten immediately or kept cold and preserved for future use by freezing or canning. Most sea animals are cooked alive.

Be willing to try everything that you can at least once. Even though it may not be a favorite of yours, you can be certain your body will benefit by the healthful vitamins, minerals and proteins which seafoods contain. While you are out in the sunshine searching for your seafood beach goodies, you are absorbing healthful vitamin D. If you wade or swim, such as when collecting abalone, the saltwater will caress, cleanse, tone and condition your body. Have you ever heard of anyone needing a tranquillizer after swimming? These are just some of the side benefits gained when you add gourmet seafoods to your diet.

No Roman feast could ever compare with what new taste treats are in store for you when you discover our riches from the ocean. Be imaginative. Try other ways of preparing these foods to fit your tastes. Basic recipes are given in the back of the book to help you get started on a wonderful new way of life — cooking these treasures from the sea.

So that future generations may continue to enjoy this beach harvest, we suggest these common sense conservation rules.

1.  Replace rocks in the position in which you found them as they serve as security for a multitude of small plants and animals.

2.  After digging clams, fill in the holes. Large mounds of sand will smother the sea life under it.

3.  Take only sea life that is plentiful and only what you need. Take only a very small amount when trying a marine plant or animal for the first time.

4.  Be informed of the state or regional fish and wildlife regulations and observe the laws regarding licenses, sizes and limits.

5.  Do not trespass on private beaches.

6.  Avoid taking animals during spawning season, especially females with eggs.

7.  Be as careful as possible when walking so as not to crush small marine creatures underfoot.

Take this book along with you to the beach and jot down where you located the seafood for future reference. Learn how the sea can be everyone's pantry. Let the tide set your table and have fun!

# LIMPETS

Limpets

Popularly called Chinese hats or coolie hats, limpets have a cone-shaped shell, tall or flattened, with no opening at tip, and all have a fleshy foot that is edible. The base is oval and open. Colors vary greatly and are often camouflaged with growths of green or brown algae (seaweed). After the body is removed for cooking the cleaned shell is very attractive either for the collector or shell crafter.

## HABITAT

Look for limpets at the highest tidal levels and where there is some surf. They cling tenaciously to rocks, other shells, stalks of kelp, sea walls or pilings, and can live for long periods of time out of water. Their main diet is algae (seaweed) which they scrape off with their rasp-like tongues (radulas). Many different species of limpets are found worldwide.

## PREPARATION AND COOKING HINTS

To release limpets from a pier, sea wall or rocks, pry up with a thin knife. Wash well. The small ones can be broiled by placing shell side down in a pan of finely-washed pea gravel or rock salt to support them. With a baster, put melted margarine on each one. Sprinkle with garlic salt and parsley, if desired. Broil for about 2 minutes. Remove stomach portion before eating if you so desire.

For large limpets, run a knife along sides to remove from shell. Cut off the top internal portion and discard. The foot part that remains may be used for chowder or put between muslin, beaten with a meat hammer, dipped in batter and fried.

In Hawaiian, the name for limpets is "opihi." The meat is dug out by using another shell. They are rubbed with coarse sea salt (red volcanic particles included) to remove slime and placed in a colander. Let set for 30 minutes. Wash and repeat process. Place in container in refrigerator. May be eaten with raw limu or honu seaweed. They may also be prepared as a soup by covering "opihi" with cold water and "miso" (salt) and bring to a boil. Remove from heat and serve.

## ABALONE

Upper left: Corrugated Abalone *Haliotis corrugata*
Lower left: Red Abalone *Haliotis rufescens*
Right: Abalone *Haliotis kamtschatkana* (showing edible foot)

The scientific family name of this shell *(Haliotidae)* means "ear shell," and is thus called in many parts of the world, whereas on the Pacific Coast the members of this family are called "abalone." They have an edible, broad, flat foot similar to limpets, but differ in form. A single shell, oval and flattened, with corrugations over the surface, it has a low spire near posterior end. One edge is thin and sharp; the other is thickened and turned under with a row of holes above it. Organs that discharge water and waste protrude from the holes. The animal discharges spawn through the respiratory vents.

## HABITAT

Being vegetarian, abalone live on rocks among seaweed from the lowest tidal level to deep water. They thrive in open, rocky coastal areas and along rocky shores of inner waters. For instance, the authors have gathered the Pinto Abalone *(Haliotis kamtschatkana)* around Vancouver Island and the San Juan Islands. The shell is often encrusted with growths that camouflage and hide a colorful exterior of maroon, green, pink, orange or black. Removal of the animal reveals a shiny, iridescent interior. Many species of abalone, or "ear shells," are found worldwide, and they are highly prized not only for food but also for shell collecting and beautiful arts and crafts.

## PREPARATION AND COOKING HINTS

The quest for the delectable abalone is a challenge and they are a real thrill to find. Not only are they scarce, but hip boots and waterproof clothing is a must for gathering them at low tide; snorkeling or scuba gear is required for the deeper levels. Unless taken by surprise, the animal and its shell is difficult to remove from the rocks, so a thin, stout pry bar is recommended.

To clean, break the meat loose from the shell by running your knife between meat and shell. Then trim off the intestines and tough dark areas. Slice across or lengthwise ¼ to ½ " thick and tenderize by pounding with a meat hammer between pieces of muslin. Dip the slices in flour and pan fry in ¼ " hot oil for 1 minute on each side. To insure tenderness, however, we recommend dipping the slices first in flour, then in slightly beaten egg and then in fine cracker or bread crumbs before frying.

We suggest preparing and eating abalone as soon as possible after gathering, for it deteriorates more rapidly than many other seafoods even if refrigerated. Freezing is not recommended as flavor is lost.

Because of the popularity of the abalones, the coastal states have set limits on the catch. The regulations on size and amount can be found in your state's fishing regulations.

Hopefully, responsible divers and other foragers will obey these limits so that our future generations will be able to gather abalones as they are enjoying them now. Use a caliber to check the sizes of your catch.

# KEYHOLE LIMPET

Rough Keyhole Limpet *Diodora aspera*

Often naturally camouflaged by living algae and encrusted with lime, this animal may elude the beachcomber. The Keyhole limpet, closely related to the abalone, is not a true limpet but is like them in appearance. It is cone-shaped and has a muscular foot on the bottom with the digestive portion under the tip of the cone. A small, nearly round opening is on the off-center tip of the rather low shell with an oval base. The exterior, usually a drab grey, sometimes has white with brown rays and numerous radiating ridges crossed by concentric lines, making a netted surface texture. It can be an attractive shell to keep after the animal is removed.

## HABITAT

Keyhole limpets are generally found at a lower tidal level than true limpets. They cling to the seaweed covered rocks of the open coast and semi-protected rocky areas. The Rough Keyhole limpet *(Diodora aspera)*, shown above, can measure 2 to 3 inches long and range from Alaska to Lower California. The largest of Keyhole limpets, Great Keyhole limpet *(Megathura crenulata)* not shown, measures 7 inches long and ranges from Monterey to Lower California. Its oval shell, with many fine radiating ridges, is nearly covered by a black mantle when found alive. Many other species are found worldwide.

## PREPARATION AND COOKING HINTS

Cut around the edge of the shell to loosen the animal. Slice off the fleshy, muscular foot, discarding the digestive organs. Also discard the commensal scale worm that is sometimes found living with the Rough Keyhole limpet. (See center limpet on page 6.) Before cooking, tenderize by placing the meat between muslin pieces and pounding with a meat hammer. Dip in a batter (see recipe section for batter suggestions) and pan fry quickly or deep fat fry. Several of the small species would be needed for each serving.

The limpet meat can be ground and used in chowder or fritters. (See recipe section.)

# MOON SNAIL

Lewis' Moon Snail (animal extended) *Polinices lewisii*

The shell is globular with a large body whorl and a short spire. It has a big, roundish opening that has a horny or calcareous operculum or trap door. Its foot, the edible part, is so enormous when extended outside that it appears impossible for the animal to draw it back into the shell. The pictured Moon snail's shell is grey-beige color, and sometimes the shell is covered with a thin, greenish algae. The largest of its species, it may reach a length of six inches.

# HABITAT

Burrowed just below the surface, Moon snails can be found by poking at smooth, low humps on muddy beaches at about zero tide level. A plunger-like object found on the beach is a Moon snail's eggs cemented together with grains of sand (see photo, upper left). The animal is carnivorous and feeds principally on clams and other bivalves. This is accomplished by wrapping the foot around its prey while the rasp-like tongue (radula) aided by a secreted enzyme, drills a hole through the shell to suck out the meat. The Moon snail shown is commonly found from British Columbia to Lower California. Many species are found worldwide.

## PREPARATION AND COOKING HINTS

Immerse live Moon snails in boiling water for about 5 minutes. Drain and place in cold water. Insert a thin, sharp knife under the umbilidus or hollow at the base of the shell far enough inside to cut the strong muscle. Remove the trap door (operculum). Insert a meat fork, twist and pull, and the animal should then come out quite easily. Slice across the foot area, discarding the digestive organs. Some people prefer to remove the dark lower area of the foot, but others feel it has the most flavor. The meat may be ground for a chowder or put between muslin and pounded with a meat hammer before rolling in flour to fry. Sprinkle with commercial meat tenderizer to insure tenderness. Moon snail slices may be dipped in batter (see recipe section) and deep fat fried. The flavor is mild, resembling that of razor clams. Some of our readers tell us that they now prefer and look for Moon snails instead of clams.

You may be able to extract the foot from the shell if you catch the snail with its foot extended <u>and</u> if you are quick and strong. Grab it tightly, twist and pull. It seems incredible that all that huge foot can fit into the seemingly small shell.

Because Moon snails do consume clams and oysters, seafood growers often destroy large quantities of this animal.

# SNAILS

Oregon Triton   *Fusitriton oregonensis*

Marine and land snails are eaten in many parts of the world and considered a great delicacy. The prolific marine snails of many species that are easily found at low tide have definite value as a source of human food.

Probably the most common are the Thais, sometimes called the Purple Snail, Dog Whelk, and Rock Purple. They are found everywhere on both the West and East Coasts. The shells, pretty to collect, come in colors of variable yellows, whites, browns, greys or striped in combinations. Some shells are smooth but others are wrinkled, short spired and thick walled. The average size is from 1 to 2 inches. The opening which is wide can be closed tightly with its horny trap door. This door is attached to the fleshy edible foot of the animal.

Not quite so common are the Triton with their hairy exterior, nor are the Neptuneas also found on both coasts. The shell of these are well worth saving and they yield a larger edible part than the small snails.

## HABITAT

Thais type snails like to live around some rocks on either the open coast or inland tide lands. They are very common intertidally. The Tritons can also be found during a low minus tide and beyond. Neptunes are found in much deeper water by diving or dredging.

Marine Snails

## PREPARATION AND COOKING HINTS

Soak the snails in fresh water for three or four hours. Scrub shells, cover with water and boil gently for 20 minutes. A little oil added to the water as you boil them will more easily release the animals from the shells. Drain and chill. Peel off horny trap door and save if you are keeping the shell, for if it is glued on a bit of cotton and replaced into the empty shell opening, it is of greater value in a collection. Pull out as much of the animal as possible. Usually the intestines stay in the shell and you are left with a nice white edible portion. Several snails are needed for a serving. Delicious dipped in melted butter, in cocktail sauce or tartar sauce. They can be ground for patties, casseroles or used as a substitute for clams in chowder. (See basic recipe pages.)

These snails are carnivorous and some are even cannibalistic when still in their egg capsules. The tiny periwinkles, some of which are black and others with a checkered design, are herbivores feeding on the algae attached to the rocks. These, too, are edible if you have the time and patience. The size is usually no bigger than 1 cm.

# CLAMS

Littleneck (top) and Washington Butters (bottom)

These tasty bivalves, members of the mollusk family, have two shells which enclose or partially enclose the soft bodies inside. All shells are calcareous but rank in hardness from the rather fragile shell of the Razor Clams to the heavy, thick shells of the Pismo and the Washington Butter Clams. All clams are edible, some more tasty than others. Do not dig clams in areas that appear polluted.

Most clams are able to close tightly or "clam up" as in the old saying. One of these is the native Littleneck Clam *(Protothaca staminea)*, also commonly called Rock Clam and Butter Clam. The color varies from cream or grey to one indistinctly mottled with browns and yellows. Concentric growth rings cross radiating ribs. The shells grow to an average of 2½ inches across, taking about ten years to reach this size.

So that the animals may clean the sand or mud out of their bodies, leave several hours in a pan or bucket of sea water. Place in the shade. Some people advocate putting a handful of cornmeal in the water. Then wash carefully with brush before steaming in a small amount of water. When shells open, they may be served with a dip of melted butter and lemon. Raw, clean clams may be frozen in the shells to steam at a later date. The water (nectar) in which the clams were steamed is delicious when seasoned with lemon and salt.

# WASHINGTON BUTTER CLAM
*(Saxidomus giganteus)*

Known also as Quahog, Coney Island, Beef Steak and the Great Oregon Clam, these bivalves have heavy, solid shells, 3 to 4 inches in length with concentric growth rings. The inside of the shell is white and grey or bluish-grey on the outside.

Look for these on rocky beaches on the minus tides. Dig where you see water coming up in squirts. The shell doesn't move, but the neck extends to the surface of the beach to feed.

## PREPARATION AND COOKING HINTS

While still alive, clean by running knife along sides to cut heavy muscle. The dark, digestive organs may be removed if you wish.

We like them fried in the half shell. To prepare, cut in half, twist to break hinge and drain on absorbent paper. In a medium heated frying pan, place margarine and lay clam, meat side down in melted fat. When brown, remove from pan and turn over. Spoon on a sauce of 2 parts A-1 sauce and 1 part lemon juice, a touch of parsley and a dash of seafood salt. Serve on the half shell. Can be ground for chowder and fritters, fried, or cut into clam strips.

In the event that the reader skipped reading the introduction, here are some important reminders when digging all clams except razors and piddocks.

After digging clams, fill in the holes. Large mounds of sand and small rocks will smother other sea creatures under it. Each animal lives at a depth that it can survive.

Take only what you need. Waste not now so that our children will want not, or that we don't deplete the resource. All clams are edible so try using the ones you find instead of leaving them on the beach to die or replace them at the depth that you found them.

Be informed of the Fish and Wildlife regulations usually posted on public beaches.

# COCKLE

Cockle Shell   *Clinocardium nuttallii*

The Cockle or Heart Shell (looks like a heart when viewing it from the side) is identifiable by the prominent, evenly-spaced ridges on the outside of the shell. The ridges come from the pointed end and radiate in a fan-like pattern ending at the edge of the shell. The Cockle lives in sand or mud just under the surface because of its short siphon, but it can move by the vigorous action of a long, muscular foot. The Cockle is found from the Bering Sea to Panama. This is a popular shell used by shell crafters.

# SURF CLAM

Surf Clam   *Spisula falcata*

The Surf Clam is not common, but it can be found from California to Georgia Straits in British Columbia. Reaching a size of 3 inches or more, the outside of the shell is nearly covered with a tannish periostracum or skin.

# SUNSET SHELL

The Sunset Shell *(Gari californica)* not shown, is found from Alaska to California in deep water. This clam may reach a size of 3 inches across. The skin or periostracum wears off with age and surf to expose pink radiating lines. If you are interested in its age, you can count the concentric growth rings.

# GEODUCK OR GUEDUC

Geoduck Clam  *Panope generosa*

On the Geoduck (goo-ee-duck) which is neither gooey nor a duck, the shell only partially covers the body and does not cover the long neck. This clam buries itself deeply in mud or sand to the depth of about 3 feet and extends its neck to the surface. Sometimes the name is spelled gueduc, a derivative for the Nisqually Indian phrase for "dig deep." Found from Alaska to Gulf of California. Dip in hot water to remove skin from neck before preparing.

The Geoduck is the largest clam in Puget Sound. They are known to weigh as much as six to ten pounds live weight. The neck of this animal is so enormous that it cannot be retracted into its shell and may extend as long as three feet. To distinguish the difference between the Horse Clam and the Geoduck, examine the shape of the shells. The anterior end of the Geoduck is nearly straight across in contrast to the rounded shell of the Horse Clam.

It takes hard work to dig Geoduck because the sand and mud collapses into the two or three foot hole necessary to reach the animal. Some foragers use a large tub or barrel with the bottom removed to support the sides. We feel that the reward is worth the effort expended.

# HORSE CLAM

Horse Clam   *Tresus nuttalli*

Another clam with a large posterior opening from which protrudes a long siphon is known by the aliases of Horse Clam, Horseneck, Blue Neck, Blue and Empire. Its neck can be distinguished from the Geoduck siphon by the tentacles on the inner edge of each siphon. The color on the siphon is black or dark green. The yellow or white outside of the shell is covered with a dark brittle periostracum.

As part of the cleaning process, dip the neck in scalding water and peel off the skin. Remove viseral material and discard. Rinse and dry clam meat on paper towels. If you are going to fry the neck, sprinkle it with a natural tenderizer and pound with a meat hammer. Better yet, grind the meat for fritters, chowder or clam casserole. Because geoduck is so rich, try combining half geoduck and half horse clams when preparing a chowder.

# PIDDOCK

Piddock Clam   *Penitella penita*

The Piddock also exposes its body between two shells that have no hinge or ligaments. This species can reach a size of about 6 inches and gaps widely at both ends. It bores into shale and clay; therefore in order to extract these clams, much beach rock must be destroyed by digging a large hole. Since the Piddock is no more flavorful than any other clam, avoid taking this species when it is possible to gather other kinds.

Examine the shell closely and you will see sharp ridges on the lower part of the shell. By rotating itself in the rock, the clam is able to scrap away enough of the rock to continue to grow. Freezing weather on an Oregon beach had cracked the rocks which exposed the clams, killing large numbers of them.

There are three species in this family, and the *P. penita* is the largest and most common in the Northwest. Its maximum length is approximately 3 inches or 7 cm.

# RAZOR CLAM

Razor Clam *Siliqua patula*

Along the sandy ocean beaches from the Arctic Ocean to California lives the very mild, white-meated Razor Clam *(Siliqua patula)*. The shiny brown shell does not completely cover the body of the animal. Limits on size, season and amounts have been imposed to keep from depleting the species. One must be quick to catch the razor clam as it is able to dig itself down into the wet sand very rapidly.

To prepare, leave clams several hours in sea water and a handful of cornmeal to allow them a chance to clean themselves. A table knife run along each side of the shell will cut the abductor muscle and then the shells may be opened and removed. With a scissors cut through two sections of the siphons of the neck if you wish to fry the whole clam. You can snip the thin skin around the digger to remove it for separate use. The dark part near the hinge may be removed but this liver is both healthful and flavorful.

The clam sack in the picture is fastened to the diggers belt to be readily accessible to drop in the catch. Some people use pails or buckets instead; however an incoming sneaky wave can easily float them away or dump them over. To dig these clams a specially designed, short handled shovel is used. Dig on the water side of the clam hole as the clams quickly retreat down on an angle towards the ocean. Many people use a cylinder device humorously called a clam gun. Place the cylinder over the hole, press down in the sand quickly holding your finger over the small hole on the top. Pull up and then release your finger. Drop the sand on the beach and look for your prize.

# JACKKNIFE CLAM

Jackknife Clam  *Solen sicarius*

This smaller, narrower clam lives in mud in protected waters. The outside of the shell is also glossy but has blunter ends rather than round ones. The meat is yellow, mottled with brown. Prepare the same as razors.

Another name for this clam is Blunt Razor Clam because of a blunt anterior end. The shiny shells are covered with a brown periostracum over a white shell. The mottled color of the animal's body may be a deterent to some foragers.

This species, like its relative the Razor Clam, is a very fast escape artist, so diggers take warning. Scuba divers say they can swim by jet propulsion after they push themselves off the bottom. Usually found on soft muddy or sandy beaches at extremely low tide levels. Jackknife Clams are rather rare although may be prevalent in fairly deep water from Puget Sound to Lower California.

# PISMO CLAM

Pismo Clam   *Tivela stultorum*

This clam has a heavy, thick shell which is white on the inside with a beige, shiny skin on the outside. This skin usually wears off as the clam matures. Its size can be as large as 8 inches across. Some have rays going across the shell from hinge to mouth area and becoming wider at the mouth.

The Pismo lives from northern California through Baja Peninsula on sandy beaches. They can be dug at a low tide or spotted in the surf when they feed. Those sold in the markets are imported from Mexico as it is illegal to dig commercially in California.

# SCALLOPS

Scallops  *Pectinidae*

For centuries the fan-shaped shell of the scallop or pectin *(Chlamys)* has inspired artists. In the Middle Ages it was used as the Crusader's badge and today is the symbol of a major oil company.

The scallop, a bivalve mollusk, is easily recognized by its shape. Existing in many colors, the shell is collected worldwide. Although all the animal is edible, just the single round muscle is usually used for fried scallops.

## HABITAT

Most scallops are free-swimming by opening and shutting its shell. The juvenile Rock Scallop is free-swimming, however, the adult is attached to rocks by the right valve of its thick shell. The presence of the boring sponge is evidenced on the exterior of the animal by a honeycomb appearance. This species is not known for being as flavorful as the free-swimming ones, but it can be found intertidally. The Rock Scallop is mainly prized for its shell. Most types are found in shallow water, preferring sheltered bays and eel grass. Skin diving with a snorkel or scuba gear is a good way to locate scallops. Take along a net and your goody bag. There are laws regulating size and limits so check each state's regulations.

Rock Scallop   *Hinnites multirugosus*

PREPARATION AND COOKING HINTS

Clean by sliding a knife between the two halves of shells and cut the muscle and the shell will open easily. The muscle can be separated from rest of animal, or the whole animal can be breaded and fried. It may be wrapped in bacon and broiled or sauteed in butter. Fresh scallop muscle, some say, are best eaten raw.

# OYSTERS

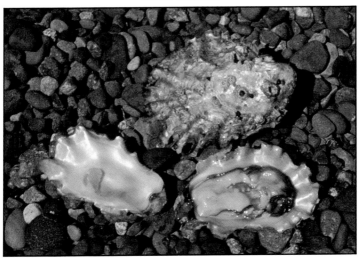

Pacific or Japanese Oyster   *Crassostrea gigas*

Many years ago the Japanese oyster *(Crassostrea gigas)* was successfully introduced, and the commercial growing of oysters became a booming Pacific Northwest industry. Spawn from commercial beds has populated bays and estuaries with so-called native oysters. This oyster has irregularly shaped shells, generally roundish to elongated, that are grey and white outside with the inside smooth and polished, and they can reach over 6 inches in length. A two part shell or bivalve, the left valve is deeper than the nearly flat right valve which fits into it.

Reportedly, the only native oyster to the Pacific Northwest is the Olympia oyster *(Ostrea lurida)* not shown, which is considered to be the ultimate in gourmet requirements. Although it was widespread on the Pacific coast, it is now uncommon and cultivation is limited. The Olympia oyster shell is small, grey in color, with little flutings. The animal inside, about the size of a man's thumbnail, is popular for eating raw.

## HABITAT

Many species of oysters are found worldwide. They like to grow intertidally where some fresh water comes into salt water, along bays and estuaries.

## PREPARATION AND COOKING HINTS

Because young oysters will fasten themselves to other oysters, removing oyster shells from the beach is prohibited in some states. Oysters can be harvested the year round, however, the meat is firmer in fall and winter months. Check the state's Fish and Game Department Rules for limits. (See hints on firming in recipe section.)

When opening oysters, thrust an oyster knife into the hinge area and slide the knife back and forth until you feel the muscle has been loosened. After opening the shell, slide the knife carefully under the meat to loosen and remove. Wash, drain and eat as desired. See recipe section for our suggestions.

# MUSSELS

Edible or Blue Mussel  *Mytilus edulis*

These black, blue or brown bivalves grow in clusters or colonies firmly attached to some solid object. The outside of the shell shows concentric growth rings and the inside has a pearly luster of the same color as the outer shell. The animal itself is an orangish color when cooked, which may discourage some people from trying this tasty seafood. The shell is more elongated than the clam. A popular edible mussel (not shown) is the California Sea mussel *(Mytilus californianus)*.

Mussels actively feed by straining microscopic plants and animals from the water through their digestive organs. If mussels are exposed to the air during a low tide, they close their shells tightly to keep their bodies and gills moist. The actual animal is much smaller than its shell, so it may serve as a host to tiny creatures, such as the pea crab; there is plenty of room and enough to eat from materials that filter in the shell while the mussel is feeding.

## HABITAT

Mussels will be found attached to pilings, rocks, anchors, and other solid objects. Do not use those attached to pilings because of the possible pollution from boats, or those mussels that are exposed to the air for long periods of time. Some states ban mussel collecting during summer months. In polluted areas, the livers of the mussels collect nitrates from the water and these nitrates could be harmful to humans. Mussels are found worldwide.

## PREPARATION AND COOKING HINTS

Since the size of the shell is deceptive, you will need to collect more mussels than you would clams per serving. Scrape the shells to remove the barnacles, seaweed and other beards (attached sissels). Wash thoroughly and discard any broken shells or open mussels. To open, place in a steamer 10 to 12 minutes. Remove from shell and serve with butter and lemon sauce.

If you wish to make a gourmet dish out of them, saute finely chopped onions in margarine or butter until tender. Add parsley and spices and 1 cup of white wine to every 4 dozen mussels. Simmer for 12 minutes and add mussels. Cover pan and let steam. Shake occasionally to open shells. When open, remove from pan and take off one shell. Use part of the liquid and thicken with flour and butter. Pour sauce over mussels and sprinkle with parsley. Serve at once.

# CHITONS OR SEA CRADLES

Small Chitons
Left to right: *Mopalia, Ischnochiton, Katharina spp.*

For millions of years the structure of these strange mollusks has remained the same. In other words they are "living fossils." They have eight plates which are usually visible on the upper surface of the animal and are held in place by a muscular "girdle." Only the Giant chiton *(Cryptochiton stelleri)* has a girdle completely covering the plates. The others have a ridge of muscle all around the upper side. All species have a smooth "foot" on the under surface which is edible.

Giant or Gumboot Chiton   *Cryptochiton stelleri*

## HABITAT

Chitons can be found almost worldwide at minus low tides or what is called the intertidal zone. The small species are attached to some type of surface, preferring undersides of rocks. Giant chitons, or gumboots are found crawling on reefs among rocks and seaweed on the beach in the low tidal zone. Small chiton never can be taken by surprise so have to be pried loose with a thin knife. Though a challenge to properly prepare the shell, they are well worth the effort to save for a collector. Clean off each section carefully, then glue back into proper position. Rub with oil to replace sheen.

Gumboot Chiton showing edible foot

## PREPARATION AND COOKING HINTS

Once sea life is collected, deterioration is rapid. Chitons, more than any other seafood, should be cleaned immediately. Pull off the smooth foot on the under surface, scrape and wash thoroughly. Small chitons will only have a bite-size piece and were usually eaten raw by the Pacific Coast Indians. For cooking, grind for either chowder or patties, or pound to tenderize, season with salt and pepper, dip in batter of egg and cracker crumbs and fry quickly.

# OCTOPUS

Octopus or Devil Fish   *Octopus apollyon*

The octopus, sometimes known as the devil fish, is a member of the mollusk family. It is the most highly developed animal without a backbone. Each of its eight appendages has a double row of suckers on the undersides. A male will have a smooth tip on the end of one tentacle.

Like a starfish, an octopus can regenerate a tentacle that has been lost with no visible harm. Healthy octopuses have been found with only four tentacles out of eight after an apparent battle with a ling cod. Their eyes are large and complex and the mouth is equipped with a sharp, parrot-like beak for tearing its food apart. It is endowed with a radula. The octopus poisons and paralyzes its prey, which is usually crustaceans and mollusks, within seconds after capture. When disturbed or for camouflage and protection, devil fish can change several different colors with great rapidity, and can discharge a cloud of ink to confuse its enemies.

The size of octopus varies with the many species found worldwide. Believed to be the largest, the Pacific octopus *(Octopus dofleini)* is found in Alaska and Puget Sound waters. One Pacific octopus captured in Alaska waters reportedly had an arm spread of 32 feet across. According to the 1979, 17th edition of Guinness Book of World Records, the largest common Pacific octopus was taken on February 18, 1973 by Donald E. Hagen, a skin diver, in lower Hood Canal, Puget Sound, Washington. It had a radial spread of 25 feet, 7 inches and weighed 118 pounds, 10 ounces. The octopus was seized at a depth of 60 feet and "wrestled" to the surface single-handed.

## HABITAT

Octopus hide in rocky crevices in subtidal or deeper water zones. In one of these, a mother octopus will lay about 200,000 eggs. She hovers protectively over the eggs and blows on them to keep the water fresh. The incubation period is approximately 50 days. The female dies after the eggs hatch; it is believed all octopuses have a short life span. Contrary to popular belief, octopus are shy creatures and not aggressive towards people.

Octopus or Devil Fish   *Octopus apollyon*

## PREPARATION AND COOKING HINTS

1.  To clean, first take out internal organs including the ink sack. Sprinkle large crystal salt on the meat and massage vigorously. This cleans the animal and helps soften it. (Table salt will have to do if a person cannot get rock salt.)

2.  Wash off salt and foam until octopus is clean.

3.  Pour enough water or white wine to barely cover the bottom of a pan. Place octopus in pot, cover and cook on *low* heat for 20 minutes or until it is done. Test for tenderness with a sharp fork. Remove from liquid, drain and cut legs and body into short strips. These strips may be served with some kind of cocktail sauce, lemon juice, shoyu sauce or butter. The people of Japanese ancestory prefer a mixture of sugar, miso and chopped green onions.

The best time to find octopus in Hawaii, where it is known as "he'e," is from July to September. Scuba divers collect them year around in Pacific Northwest waters.

# SQUID

Opalescent Squid   *Loligo opalescens*

A relative of the octopus, nautilus and cuttlefish, the squid is actually a marine mollusk or sea shell. It has no shell, but a shell-like "pen" grown in the muscles of its tube-shaped body. Squid have ten arms or tentacles extending from the head with two arms longer than the rest. They use the suction cups on these arms to seize and hold their prey. The head, located at the base of the tentacles, has a strong, horny beak capable of cutting up or tearing apart shrimp, crabs or fish on which it feeds; it also has two highly developed eyes. The body, beneath the head and tentacles, has two fins at the tail end. By filling a cavity in its body with water and forcing it out through its tube-like body, squid can propel themselves backwards very rapidly. They can travel forward by beating their flexible fins. A squid, like an octopus, can change color to match its surroundings, especially when alarmed. To further confuse its enemies, it may eject ink or sepia as it darts away to hide. Squid vary in length from a few inches to over 40 feet long. The Giant squid is the largest living invertebrate (animal without backbone) in the world, and still somewhat a mystery to scientists. Squid terrified old-time seafarers who called it "kraken." Among Norsemen, it became the infamous monster of many an ancient legend.

## HABITAT

Many species of squid are found worldwide. They prefer the open ocean, traveling in massive schools near the surface and conversely, in water 200 to 500 feet deep or more. However, some species do inhabit inshore waters and are occasionally seen by divers. For instance, the Pacific Bob-tailed squid *(Rossia pacifica)* lives in shallow coastal waters from Alaska to Baja California, in eastern Russia and around Japan. Since this species is a bottom dweller, it can be captured by agile scuba divers. Vast amounts of squid are harvested commercially by using nets or lures called jigs. The delicately flavored meat is considered gourmet fare in China, Japan, Korea, Italy, Spain, Portugal and in recent years, the United States. Japan alone harvests more than 600 million tons of squid every year.

Bob-tailed Squid   *Rossia pacifica*

## PREPARATION AND COOKING HINTS

Skin the entire squid including the tentacles. The suction cups on the tentacles usually come off with the skin. Cut off the head, leaving the tentacles attached, if possible. Pull out the thin, flat "pen" (also called cuttlebone in some species) and remove the internal organs. Rinse well. The hollow tube may now be stuffed (see recipe section). We also recommend slicing the squid crosswise into 1 inch slices, dipping the slices and tentacles in "Light and Airy Batter" (see recipe section). Deep fat fry until lightly brown (about 2 minutes) at 400 degrees. These are delicious served hot on toothpicks and dipped in tarter sauce or any of your favorite seafood sauces for hors d'oeuvres.

# SEA CUCUMBER

Large Red Sea Cucumber  *Strichopus californicus*

A member of the spiny-skinned animals *(Echinodermata)*, the sea cucumber has rows of large tube feet on the underside and large, conical-shaped spines on the upper side. These animals are a beautiful orange-red color with a mouth on one end and an anus on the other. Its defense mechanism throws out its internal organs so that the attacker is so busy eating or disentangling himself that the cucumber is able to slip away unnoticed. It can repeat this effective defense process for perhaps four times throughout its life. A full grown cucumber may be 15 inches long and about 4 inches around.

# HABITAT

Named the "dandelion of the sea" because they are so plentiful, sea cucumbers usually live in deeper waters beyond the lowest tide level. They can occasionally be netted when they swim near the surface of the water, or more likely, gathered by scuba divers. Sea cucumbers are found worldwide.

Cucumber showing edible muscles

## PREPARATION AND COOKING HINTS

Drop the animal in boiling water for 1 minute to firm up the tissue and make it easier to handle. Remove from the water and drain. Slice off both ends. Slit the body lengthwise, using a sharp knife or scissors. Rinse off the visceral material. Slide a finger under the center of the white muscle and work towards the two ends to remove. These five, long muscles can be cut into bite-size pieces. Dip into flour with seasonings and fry 1 minute on each side. Serve as hors d'oeuvres. The entire skin with the muscle may be fried if desired although it may be chewy. Use muscles for chowder or fritters as the flavor resembles a mild clam.

Some Orientals first boil, dry and then smoke the body walls to be used in soup. Indians of the Pacific Northwest were known to hang and dry the body walls to preserve them. Sea cucumbers are known and considered gourmet fare in many parts of the world as "Beche-de-mer" or "caterpillar of the sea."

# SEA URCHINS

Top: *Stronglocentrotus franciscanus*
Bottom left: *Stronglocentrotus purpuratus*
Bottom right: *Stronglocentrotus droebachiensis*

Are you ready for caviar that you can collect on the beach? From a sea urchin you can scoop out the eggs or gonads with an index finger by circumventing the body through the mouth cavity. Urchins are another member of the spiny-skinned animals "Echinodermata."

Sea urchins have spines for protection and tube feet for locomotion. On the underside is a mouth with five teeth-like plates. When this portion is removed, it resembles an old Greek lantern and is named Aristotle's lantern, as he was the first scientist to describe it. The size at maturity ranges from 3 to 5 inches across, depending on the species. Algae and minute organisms are the main food consumed by the sea urchin. Urchins have become a menace to commercial kelp beds in California by eating through the stalks of the young plants. These plants then wash up on the beach and die. The natural enemy of the urchin is the sea otter.

## HABITAT

Some sea urchins are found in colonies at the lowest tide level. Others live in rocks where they constantly turn to scrape away the rock to keep it large enough for their growth. All species are supposedly edible, but some tropical ones have poisonous spines. To protect the hands, use thick gloves when collecting.

## PREPARATION AND COOKING HINTS

For ease in handling, drop animal in boiling water for 2 minutes. Remove, drain and crack lightly from the underside to remove the internal parts. The eggs and gonads (edible portions) can be easily separated from the intestinal organs by washing carefully. Those who relish this delicacy usually spread the eggs (roe) and gonads on thick bread or crackers. The brighter the orange color, the better the flavor. To the authors, the taste resembles that of an under-ripe peach or a papaya. A squirt of lemon or lime enhances the flavor.

From Australia comes the report that live urchins are thrown into an open fire until the spines burn. They are then removed, cracked open and consumed while steamy. Pacific Northwest Indians ate sea urchins for food and medicinal purposes. Sea urchins are relished by many countries in Asia and known as "Wana" in Hawaii. The Hawaiians shake the urchins in wire baskets or burlap bags to break off the spines; then they are rubbed against a rock to complete the process. They break a hole in the top side to remove what they call tongue. Mix this with garlic or hot peppers and store in the refrigerator. Hawaiians say to collect during periods of lowest tides for fullest, sweetest tongue.

# GOOSE BARNACLES

Goose Barnacle *Pollicipes polymerus*

This species, sometimes called the Gooseneck barnacle, may have received its name because of the leather-like peduncle or stalk that resembles the long neck of a goose, but more likely the name originated from a zoology book written in 1597 in which the author testified that baby geese fell feet first from the head of these creatures and into the water. To the authors, this species of barnacle looks similar to a horse's hoof.

The crown of the animal may reach the width of an inch or more across and nearly 2 inches high. The crown consists of many nail-like plates. Between the four largest plates, two on each side, come curled, yellow appendages which literally sweep the water for small sea creatures to consume. The brownish-red peduncle, the edible part of the animal, may reach a length of 6 inches.

All barnacles are edible, such as those shown below, but the Acorn are so difficult to remove from the shell part that it is hardly worth the effort.

Acorn Barnacle   *Balanus glandula*

## HABITAT

Gooseneck barnacles are usually found in regions where the surf is strong, but where shelter can be found like in rocky crevices. They are usually exposed at about half-tide mark. Some specimens have been found growing on whales and on ships. The distribution is worldwide.

## PREPARATION AND COOKING HINTS

Cook as soon as possible after gathering. If you must store for any length of time, keep in cool sea water. Avoid pulling from rocks or other material on which they are growing so the barnacles will stay alive. When ready to prepare, wash carefully in fresh water especially the area where it had been attached. Cover the bottom of a steamer pan with water. When the water begins to boil, place whole barnacles in upper portion of steamer pan, cover and leave for 20 minutes. At the end of the steaming period, remove from pan. When cool enough to handle, remove the crown part and the leather-like skin and discard. The bite size portion you will have left is worth the effort. The meat, red in color, has somewhat the consistency of crab, but is more flavorful. These pieces can be dipped in butter or lemon and seasoned with a seafood salt.

# SHRIMP

Coon-striped Shrimp  *Pandalus danae*

This circus-looking animal has red stripes along the sides of his body and across the long antennae and legs. The beak or rostrum has sharp spines to be avoided when you are cleaning it. His dance is as graceful as a ballerina, but he has an aggressive and gluttonous personality. The size from end of rostrum to end of tail may reach 6 inches, almost the size of prawns, and his antennae may be equally as long as the body.

## HABITAT

Coon-striped shrimp are usually found in waters that range from 50 to 200 feet deep. Immature shrimp feed in the shallower waters. Many different species are found throughout the world. Prawns, similar to large shrimp, can be substituted in most recipes.

Shrimp are harvested by dropping a trap which contains powerful smelling bait, such as cat food or fish heads, to the bottom of the shrimping area. Always check the fisheries' department regulations and the area's seasonal and poundage limits.

## PREPARATION AND COOKING HINTS

Most markets sell whole shrimp by the pound so figure on over fifty percent waste. If you trap them yourself, drop live into boiling, salted water (add garlic or other herbs if you wish) and simmer about 12 minutes, depending on the size or amount. Remove from heat, pour off water and cool immediately by covering with ice cubes. When cool enough to handle, hold the body firmly and break off the head. Next, peel off the shell. You are now ready to dip the cleaned shrimp into cocktail sauce, to make a delicious salad or casserole, or to dip in batter and deep fat fry. (See recipe section.)

Another method of preparation is to break off the heads while still alive to use for deep fat frying or for freezing in brine. To cook frozen raw shrimp, bring the water to a boil, cook 20 seconds, remove and chill immediately. Raw shrimp are delicious sauteed in a small amount of oil with your favorite seasonings (be inventive), or dipped in batter and deep fat fried.

In Hawaii, small black shrimp known as "opae Kai," are consumed raw when combined with Hawaiian chili peppers, nori (red seaweed), and crushed kukui nuts or they simply fry them in oil.

# CALIFORNIA SPINY LOBSTER

California Spiny Lobster  *Panulirus interruptus*

Because this animal lacks claws, it is not a true lobster hence its other name, the California crayfish. Two long antennae point backwards from the head of the animal in contrast to the spines on its back area which point forward. Truly beautiful when alive, this lobster possesses a deep red carapace or shell, covered with bright blue phosphorescent spots. A very large specimen may be up to 3 feet long and weigh up to 30 pounds. Like crabs, lobsters eat either plants or animals living or dead. Generally spiny lobsters migrate to the deeper waters during the winter and return closer to the shore when the weather gets warmer.

## HABITAT

This lobster is found from northern California through the west coast of Mexico and other waters of the Pacific. Most large specimens are found in subtidal areas but smaller ones can be gathered in rocky tide pools at a low minus tide. Check with the California Department of Fish and Game for the season, size and the methods available for capturing this delicious crustacean.

## PREPARATION AND COOKING HINTS

Boil entire animal for 15 minutes for a small lobster and up to 40 minutes for a very large one. When cool enough to handle, break off tail from the body by arching the back until it breaks. Cut through the underside of the tail lengthwise to split open and remove the meat. Serve with melted herbal butter. You may prefer to add fresh dill or dill seeds to the boiling water before dropping in the lobster. If lobster is frozen, reduce the cooking time.

# RED TUNA CRAB

Red Tuna Crab  *Pleuroncodes planipes*

This strange crustacean has a body which resembles a lobster, six legs, a head like a shrimp, and two crab-like pincers on the ends of two long legs, which extend forward. The abdomen, where the female carries her eggs until they hatch, is curled beneath the body. When alive, their color is pinkish brown, which changes into orange after cooking. Sometimes as many as three dozen will find their way into a shrimp trap. They range in size from four to 6½ inches from the end of the pincers to the end of the tail. The eyes are on stalks between which extends a sharp beak.

## HABITAT

Not beach dwellers, these crabs are found in waters from 50 to 200 feet deep, thus they are frequently found in crab and shrimp pots. They appear to be most plentiful at the shallower depths of Hood Canal and other Northwest waters and as far south as southern California.

## PREPARATION AND COOKING HINTS

Cook the whole animal about 10 minutes in simmering water. Garlic or onions may be added to the cooking water. Remove from the heat, drain and cool. Break off the head and discard. The edible meat is in the tail portion, but it takes patience and time to extract it from the shell. Applying pressure on both ridges on the underside will crack the shell so it can be peeled off. Use meat in cocktails and salads, or combined with crab or shrimp meat in recipes. For a delightful snack, melt a third cup of butter or margarine, add one teaspoon parsley flakes and one-fourth teaspoon garlic powder. Add crab and heat thoroughly. Serve on toothpicks.

# CRABS

Crabbing is well-known worldwide as a family sport and an important commercial industry. Crabmeat, a delight to most palates, makes crabs the least incredible of our sea life edibles. Despite their fierce combative dispositions, as compared to a meek octopus or a timid sea cucumber, they are highly prized by a lover of seafood.

# DUNGENESS

Dungeness Crab    *Cancer magister*

The Dungeness Crab is the most famous and important crab on the West Coast of the United States. It is bluish-brown on the back when alive, and light yellow underneath. It can grow to a maximum width of 10 or 12 inches. Average life span is 8 to 12 years with sexual maturity reached in 4 or 5 years. Only males can be used for consumption. Check state regulations yearly for legal size and limits.

Although nicknamed Dungeness for a locality in the State of Washington, it is found all the way from Alaska to Baja California. It likes sandy and muddy bottoms of inland waters and open sea. The Dungeness can be sometimes found in shallow inland waters and ocean lagoons during clam tides. Successful bay crabbing is done with a boat by setting fish-baited traps. Scuba diving in a likely area can yield the diver a tasty Dungeness.

# RED ROCK

Red Rock  *Cancer productus*

Not taken commercially, people should try to catch more of this excellent edible crab, for there is no limit on the size or amount taken. It can get almost as large as the Dungeness but has a harder shell. Coloring is brick red on the back and light beneath with dark tips on the claws. The Rock Crab, though smaller than the Dungeness, can yield as much meat as its larger cousin because of its larger claws.

## HABITAT

The Red Rock is found only from Vancouver Island to Lower California. This species moves into rocky intertidal areas. We have dug them when clam digging. They are successfully taken with baited traps.

# PUGET SOUND KING

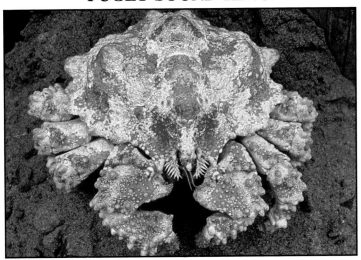

Puget Sound King Crab  *Lopholithodes mandtii*

Very delicious, this one is not well-known and should not be confused with the commercially caught Alaska King Crab. Puget Sound King crab can be identified by its purple nubs on brilliant orange-red surfaces.

## HABITAT

Puget Sound Kings have been found by divers around Vancouver Island, Straits of Juan de Fuca, San Juan Islands and Puget Sound. They live subtidally with divers taking them from rocky bottoms of depths from 30 to 50 feet.

These crabs along with its relatives the Box Crabs are the largest in our Puget Sound area. They have been found to be as large as 11 plus inches or 30 cm. in diameter across the carapace.

Although the adult is rarely found intertidally juveniles may be found at an extremely low tide. The young are bright orange or red with lavender or purple tinges.

When the Puget Sound King Crab feels threatened, it tucks its legs under its body and becomes rigid and box like. This crab lacks the foramin (holes) between the claws and first pair of walking legs. Divers report that these crabs congregate in certain areas.

# BOX CRAB

Box Crab  *Lopholithodes foraminatus*

This crab is similar to the Puget Sound King with its orange-red coloring and its ability to fold its legs against the body, forming an armored box. It has a heavy external skeleton covered with bumps and nubs. Each front pincer has a circular hole which allows water to enter the gill chamber. The Puget Sound King does not have these holes.

The abdominal plate is so soft and floppy that it scrapes on the bottom thus impeding the forward motion. Because of this and the heavy carapace, the Box and Puget Sound King Crabs are not as mobile as other species of crabs so they must resort to fooling their enemies by "boxing up".

The Box Crab feeds on organic material that filters down to the bottom of Puget Sound and that may be to depths up to 50 feet or more.

## HABITAT

Located in waters of the Northwestern United States and Puget Sound, this creature lives below the lowest tide line in sand and mud. It is caught quite often by divers. Cleaning and cooking hints in recipe section.

# SEA LETTUCE

Sea Lettuce   *Ulva lactuca*

For a new taste treat, collect *(Ulva lactuca)*, commonly called sea lettuce, which resembles the land plant, leaf lettuce. Of all the algae, this is one of the most easily recognized and belongs to the green algae group *(Chlorophyta)*. To find, look for bright green, thin, translucent, single blades with a very small, disk-shaped holdfast. A number of irregularly-shaped blades grow from the holdfast, resembling a loose head of leaf lettuce.

## HABITAT

Sea lettuce usually grows in the upper intertidal zone. It is attached to rocks, shells, or other plants, and can be seen free-floating in quiet bays, lagoons and mud flats. It breaks loose during rough water and can be gathered from the top of the water afterwards. Sea lettuce is found from Alaska to Chile, and in other parts of the world.

Wash the lettuce carefully to remove all sand and other substances. Drop lettuce into a pan of boiling, salted water and cook about 2 minutes. Remove from heat, drain, and serve with butter, seafood salt or, if preferred, a little vinegar. Another species, *(Enteromorpha intestinalis)*, which looks like stringy sea lettuce, will serve just as well and may even be a little more tender.

Shred raw sea lettuce into small pieces to add to a tossed salad. You may find it a bit chewy, but it will make your salad look more appetizing and add healthful minerals.

# SUGAR WRACK

Sugar Wrack   *Laminaria saccharina*

Sugar Wrack, scientifically called *(Laminaria saccharina)*, is just one of many species of seaweed belonging to the group of large alga *(Phaeophyta)* which are also called kelp. This species has a long yellow-brown blade of variable lengths from 3 to 6 feet, and widths approximately one-fourth of the length. The solid stipe or stem is short, only 1 to 3 inches long, and the oval blade is smooth, except for variable large ripples. The blade feels sticky to the touch as it contains mucilage. A holdfast of root-like structures anchors the plant to the substratum. Sugar Wrack receives its name because it contains a sugar alcohol called mannitol.

## HABITAT

This species of kelp, along with its many relatives, is found fastened to rocks, piling and other plants in the lower intertidal to upper subtidal areas. A perennial, it is one of the most common seaweeds in the Pacific Northwest. The distribution of Sugar Wrack is from Alaska through Oregon and along northern California.

## PREPARATION AND COOKING HINTS

If possible, gather the young growth of Sugar Wrack in spring and early summer. Wash the freshly gathered seaweed carefully in fresh water to remove any debris and eggs of small marine animals that may have been deposited on it. It is now ready to use in our suggested recipes (see recipe section), or dry for future use. Dried Sugar Wrack can be eaten as snacks like peanuts. The sugar it contains, called fucose, is not harmful to diabetics as it does not raise the sugar level of the blood.

Large seaweeds or kelps are mostly harvested commercially for the alginic acids they contain. Since thirteen of the fourteen elements essential for the balance of metabolic functions of the human body are contained in kelp, some form of kelp should be part of our daily diet.

# BULL KELP

Bull or Ribbon Kelp   *Nereocystis luetkeana*

One of the largest seaweeds known, Bull kelp *(Nereocytis luetkeana)* belongs to the brown *(Phaeophyta)* group of alga. The long whip-like stem, resembling a large snake or bull whip, ends with a hollow bulb from which grows long, strap-shaped fronds called blades. Offshore the bulb with its trailing fronds acts as a float for the long stem which is anchored to the substrata by a huge holdfast. This species of kelp grows more than a foot a day during the summer months. Some plants reach over 100 feet in length! Northwest Indians used to dry and oil the long stipes for fishing lines.

Kelp is generally called "kombu" by the Japanese and as "limu" in Hawaii. Unknowingly, you are already consuming kelp as part of your regular diet. Algin, which is derived from kelp, is used in puddings, ice cream, chocolate milk, mayonnaise and other foods that need a smoothing agent. Drug items such as toothpaste, shaving cream and pharmaceutical products rely on algin as well as many building products.

Seaweeds, especially kelp, contain a richer source of potassium, iodine and many other minerals, than land vegetables. Since these minerals are needed by the body for good health, a good way to get them is by learning to use seaweed in your soups and other dishes. For those unable to get fresh or dried seaweed, kelp tablets are available at your pharmacy.

If you grow your own vegetables and fruits, try using seaweed as a fertilizer to insure that your food will be richer in minerals.

In Alaska, divers harvest edible kelp upon which the herring have spawned during the last couple of weeks in April. These are processed as salted herring eggs of kelp, which are known as "Kazunoko Kombu" in Japan, where it is marketed.

According to David P. Chynoweth of the Bioconversion Research Institute of Gas Technology, a potential use for kelp is to provide a continuous, almost unlimited source of biomass for the future production of a non-polluting substitute for natural gas.

## HABITAT

Beds of Bull kelp are common along the rocky, coastal waters from Alaska to California. The plants usually grow in upper subtidal areas of strong surf to deeper waters, but occasionally they can be found at the very lowest intertidal level. Some kelp beds off the California coasts are protected by law, so check with the Fish and Game Department before collecting. The offshore groves of kelp provide a natural habitat for marine fishes, sea urchins and sea otters. Often the young plants are destroyed after the urchins eat through the stipe, but the otters in turn feast on the sea urchins.

Other species of kelp, such as *(Macrocystis integrifolia)*, *(Fucua spp.)*, *(Laminaria spp.)*, and *(Alaria spp.)* are also found along rocky, coastal regions. Kelp is harvested commercially from the California coast, Japan, and other parts of the world.

## PREPARATION AND COOKING HINTS

For eating, try to cut a living plant or one that has only recently broken off and floated to shore. Use stipes no longer than 15 feet long and not more than 3 inches in diameter. It must break crisply to be fresh enough to use for pickles. See recipe section.

# TURKISH TOWEL

Turkish Towel   *Gigartina*

A member of the red group of alga *(Rhodophyta)*, Turkish Towel is a species of *(Gigartina)* that is easily recognized. The plant has a single, large, irregularly shaped blade with numerous short projections on both sides of the surface that resemble a turkish towel. The size and shape of the blade varies, being 8 to 12 inches long or more. From a short stipe, the blade widens gradually to become broadly rounded at the tip. The disk-shaped holdfast usually supports more than one blade. Young specimens are yellowish to bright red with a glossy surface. Older specimens are a duller, dark red to purplish, and they appear iridescent under water. The many *(Gigartina)* species of seaweed are close relatives of Irish Moss *(Chondrus crispus)* or carrageen, and can be used similarly.

## HABITAT

Turkish Towel grows on rocks in the lower intertidal to subtidal zones. Common on Washington shores, its distribution is from British Columbia, Canada to California.

## PREPARATION AND COOKING HINTS

Gather only young plants, if possible. Wash well in fresh water, being careful to remove any encrustations or eggs deposited by small marine animals. Turkish Towel may be used fresh or dried in entrees, desserts and even cough syrups to relieve coughs and colds. See the recipe section for our suggestions, or use your imagination with this versatile seaweed.

# TIPS ON COLLECTING SEAWEED

1.  All seaweeds deteriorate rapidly after they are harvested if not kept cool.

2.  Do not transport seaweed in buckets of water.

3.  When gathering seaweed, be prepared to place each species in a separate container, if possible. Plastic bags are ideal if the bag of seaweed is placed in a cooler or refrigerator as soon as you leave the beach. Moist seaweed in a plastic container will keep up to 3 days in the refrigerator.

4.  If a cooler or refrigeration is not available, and since most are harvested during spring and summer months, try nature's way of preserving them. Spread the salt-water rinsed seaweed on logs or dry sand at about the high tide level. After a few hours, it should be dry enough to pack in dry containers for transporting home, where it may need further drying. Store in a dry place.

5.  When reconstituting beach dried or commercially packaged seaweed, thoroughly rinse to remove all sand and debris. See the recipe section.


# EDIBLES IN INCREDIBLE INDIAN STYLE

To steam open clams, take a suggestion from our early Americans and use seaweed. The Indians dug a hole, placed a few large rocks in the bottom and made a fire in the pit to heat the rocks thoroughly. After the fire was out, the clams were put into the hole, covered with seaweed and then dirt. The clams were steamed in their juices for about an hour before uncovering to eat. Those clams not eaten were preserved by smoking. The seaweed does add flavor to the clams and can be done in the kitchen by placing clams between layers of seaweed in a large pan and steaming for 10 to 15 minutes or until clams are all open. When available, our preference in seaweed would be *(Fucus)*, commonly called Rockweed, or Popping Wrack although other species of seaweed would be satisfactory. If the seaweed does not contain enough water, add a little to the bottom of the pan. This method of steam cooking in pits has also been used for salmon.

The Klallam Indian women used seaweed for cooking limpets also. When they found a large flat rock covered with limpets, they laid seaweed on the rock and covered the seaweed with hot stones. The limpets loosen their hold on the rock as they cook. They may then be eaten right on the beach or scraped off and taken home.

According to materials gathered from the Ozette excavation near Neah Bay, Washington, the Makahs reportedly ate crab, clams, chitons, mussels, limpets, gooseneck barnacles and sea anemones.

Indians have long considered the Grunts, also known as Singing Fish or Midshipman, a delicious sweet treat. They were boiled right on the beach. Grunts average about 12 inches long, have a broad head, no scales and a body covered with round shiny spots called photophores. These fish are found beneath rocks in the intertidal zone during spring and early summer when the female Grunt comes ashore to lay her eggs. After the eggs are laid, the male then guards the eggs until they become free-swimming, and as a warning, he makes a humming sound when disturbed. This defenseless fish should not be taken during the spring and summer months when they are spawning.

Blennies, sometimes called Prickleback, and mistakenly thought to be eels, were also a special beach treat. These eel-like fish have small, pointed heads and long dorsal fins that run into the tail fins. They are commonly found in the intertidal zone, where they can live for hours in their cool, moist hiding places beneath rocks. Because of the strong fishy odor the Blenny emits when frying, soak first in a solution of 4 parts salt water to 1 part vinegar. Garlic or spices may be added to the solution, if desired. After a couple of hours, dry and deep fat fry with or without batter. (See recipe section for batter.)

Olachen or Candlefish cooked with Sea Lettuce is delicious reports a Makah friend of ours. The Candlefish is supposedly so oily that it will burn like a candle when dried. Olachen, like smelt, travel in schools and can be scooped into nets while standing about knee-high in water. Try the cooking hints for Blennies if you are lucky enough to net some Olachen.

# RECIPE LIST

# NEPTUNE'S CLAM NECTAR

After steaming clams, carefully strain the nectar that remains in the pot to remove any sand or bits of shell. Heat slowly until it just comes to a simmering boil. Serve before meal with small bite size rolls for appetizers. May add dash of lemon and sprinkle of ground sea lettuce to nectar, if desired.

# BISQUE (Thick Soup)

½ lb. flaked crab, lobster or
  ground-up abalone
½ cup dry sherry
1 10¾ oz. can condensed
  tomato soup

1 10¾ oz. can condensed
  green pea soup
1¼ cups Half and Half cream
¾ tsp. curry powder,
  chopped parsley or paprika

Marinate seafood in sherry for 30 minutes. In a saucepan blend together soups, Half and Half and seasonings. Heat slowly, stirring constantly but do not boil. Add seafood and sherry and heat through. Serve immediately sprinkled with parsley or paprika. Serves 4.

# OYSTER STEW

For every pint of oysters, use the following ingredients: 3 cups milk and cream (as rich as you prefer), ¼ cup butter or margarine, 1½ teaspoons salt (seafood salt may be substituted), ½ teaspoon monosodium glutamate and pepper.

Pick over oysters carefully to remove any particles of shells. Scald milk and set aside. In a saucepan, melt butter. Add oysters with their liquid. Simmer 3 minutes or until oysters are plump and edges begin to curl. Add oyster mixture to milk and seasoning. Heat but do not boil. Serve with oyster crackers. Serves about 4.

# BOUILLABAISSE

This is a French soup of fish and shellfish which may be improvised to suit the type of seafood you have available.

You may use more than one kind of white fish, shellfish such as shrimp, crab or lobster, and mollusks which include clams, oysters and mussels.

In a large pan, brown leeks or onions in oil. Add finely chopped tomatoes and a small amount of garlic. In another pan brown fish fillets which are cut into small pieces. Do not scorch the butter or margarine you are using to saute the fish. Add fish stock to the large kettle and add the fish. Add herbs such as parsley, thyme and basil. Let come to a simmer for about 8 minutes and add cooked shellfish. When it again comes to a boil, add some white wine and do not let it boil again. The fish stock may be obtained ahead of time by boiling the fish head and bones. With this soup, improvise until you are satisfied with the results.

# TARTAR SAUCE

*To serve with fish and all other seafood*

1 cup mayonnaise or salad
  dressing (personal choice)
⅔ cup pickle relish
1 tsp. chopped parsley
½ tsp. chopped chives

½ tsp. salt
½ tsp. pepper
2 tsp. chopped capers
  (optional, if you like it hot)

Mix all ingredients together. Store in airtight container in refrigerator.

# LOUIS SAUCE (For Shrimp or Crab)

1 cup mayonnaise
¼ cup French dressing or
  Thousand Island dressing
¼ cup catsup or chili sauce

1 tsp. horseradish
1 tsp. Worcestershire sauce
Salt and coarsely ground pepper

Mix mayonnaise, French dressing, catsup, horseradish and Worcestershire together; add salt and pepper to taste and refrigerate until until serving time.

# COCKTAIL SAUCE

½ cup catsup
3 Tbsp. lemon juice
1 Tbsp. horseradish
Celery or garlic salt
(If desired, add minced celery)

2 drops Tabasco or other
  red pepper sauce
¼ tsp. salt (optional)
2 tsp. Worchestershire Sauce

Mix all ingredients. May be made ahead of time, but keep covered.

# LIGHT & AIRY BATTER

1 egg, separated
½ cup sifted flour
1 Tbsp. cornstarch

½ tsp. salt
½ tsp. pepper
½ cup cold water

In a small bowl, beat egg white until stiff enough to form peaks. Set aside. Sift flour, cornstarch, salt and pepper. In another bowl beat egg yolk and water until frothy. Continue beating this mixture while gradually adding flour mixture. Beat until smooth. Fold in beaten egg white into flour mixture. Chill batter for at least 1 hour. Stir occasionally when tempura cooking.

# BASIC FRITTER BATTER (For Deep Fat Frying)

2 eggs
1 cup milk
1 cup all-purpose flour

1 tsp. baking powder
1 tsp. salt
2 tsp. melted shortening

Put eggs in small mixing bowl and beat for 1 minute. Add milk, flour, baking powder, salt and shortening. Fry clams, scallops, crabs or any sea life desired this way in fat for 2 to 3 minutes at 400 degrees.

# BASIC FRENCH FRY

2 eggs, beaten
¾ cup milk

Salt and pepper mixed
   with flour
Fine bread crumbs, sifted

Roll freshly cleaned seafood, such as oysters, clams, sea cucumber, shrimp, etc. in seasoned flour. Dip floured seafood in combined egg and milk mixture. Drain excess liquid and roll in bread crumbs. Gently shake off crumbs. Fry in deep fat 3 or 4 minutes (less if seafood is small) at 375 to 400 degrees.

# OYSTER HELPFUL HINT

To firm oysters in the reproductive spring and summer months, you can either parboil for approximately 2 minutes or drop into ice water about 10 minutes before preparing.

# FRIED OYSTERS

Dip opened oysters in egg and milk mixture, roll in cornmeal and set aside for 5 minutes. Fry in hot oil until brown and crisp. Some people prefer using whole wheat flour instead of corn meal.

# OYSTER CASSEROLE

Crush soda crackers until you have about 3 cups. Melt 2 cubes margarine and stir in the cracker crumbs. Place about half the mixture on the bottom of an 8 x 10 inch pan. Drain oysters and place on top of crumbs. If you prefer, cut large oysters. After you have made a single layer of oysters, sprinkle with seafood seasoning or salt, parsley and pepper. Place the remaining crumbs over oysters and bake for about 1 hour or more at 375 degrees. Crackers should be crisp and oysters firm when dish is ready to serve.

# OYSTER DRESSING

Add 1 cup drained oysters and 1 teaspoon of seafood seasoning to every quart of your favorite bread stuffing. If the oysters are large, you may want to cut them into smaller pieces. The addition of parsley and celery enhances the flavor of the oysters.

# ALMOND OYSTERS

| | |
|---|---|
| ¼ tsp. nutmeg | 2 Tbsp. butter or margarine |
| ¼ tsp. ginger | 3 Tbsp. flour |
| ¾ cup oyster liquor | ½ cup blanched almonds |
| ½ cup chicken broth or stock | 1 Tbsp. parsley and pimento |
| 1 qt. carefully schucked oysters | Salt and pepper to taste |

Combine the first four ingredients in a saucepan. Simmer for 4 minutes, add the oysters and cook over low heat until the edges begin to curl. Remove the oysters and keep warm. Strain the liquid through a tea strainer to remove any bits of shell.

In a saucepan melt butter, gradually blend in flour. Pour in liquid slowly while stirring and cook until sauce has thickened. Add the parsley and pimento, then almonds and oysters; heat, but do not boil. Add salt and pepper to taste. Serve on buttered toast or English muffins.

# OYSTER QUICHE

1 unbaked 9 inch pastry shell
4 eggs, beaten
2 cups Half and Half
(or use 1 large can of
evaporated milk, adding
water to make 2 cups
1 Tbsp. flour
2 Tbsp. cooking sherry

½ tsp. dried tarragon
Dash of paprika
1 Tbsp. finely chopped chives
½ tsp. salt
2 cans smoked oysters,
drained and chopped (smoked
clams or mussels may be
substituted)

Beat eggs; add milk, flour, sherry, tarragon, paprika, chives and salt. Mix until well blended. Arrange drained, chopped oysters on the pastry shell. Pour egg and milk mixture over the oysters and bake at 375 degrees for about 35 minutes or until an inserted knife comes out clean.

# OYSTER-CRAB BAKE

1 pint raw oysters
1 pint crab meat
3 Tbsp. butter
3 Tbsp. flour
⅓ cup oyster broth
1 cup lukewarm milk
¼ tsp. nutmeg
¼ tsp. each salt and pepper
2 Tbsp. butter

1 egg yolk
½ cup cream (undiluted
evaporated milk may be
substituted)
3 Tbsp. grated Swiss cheese
1 cup fresh mushrooms
(optional)
¼ cup Parmesan cheese
Paprika

Simmer oysters in 1 cup water or in their own liquid for about 5 minutes. Reserve ⅓ cup of oyster broth for sauce. Canned oysters may be substituted for fresh ones.

Make a cream sauce by melting 3 Tbsp. butter, stirring into butter 3 Tbsp. flour and cooking this until bubbly. Remove from heat and gradually add oyster broth and lukewarm milk; continue cooking, stirring constantly until smooth and thickened. Gradually add the egg yolk that has been beaten with the cream and the nutmeg, pepper and salt. Stirring constantly bring sauce just to a boil. Remove from heat, add butter and cheese and reheat carefully, but do not boil.

Butter 4 individual casseroles or an 8 or 9 inch baking dish. Place a layer of oysters, evenly divided in fourths, in each casserole or in the bottom of the baking dish. Spoon a layer of cream sauce over the oysters, then a layer each of mushrooms and crab meat and another layer of cream sauce. Sprinkle with Parmesan cheese and paprika. Bake at 400 degrees for 20 minutes.

## PICKLED SCALLOPS

½ cup olive oil
2 onions, medium size
½ cup vinegar
½ tsp. pepper

2 small chili peppers
1 lb. raw scallops
1 tsp. salt
¼ tsp. dry mustard

Wash scallops and slice ½ inch thick if large ones. Drain, pat dry. In 2 tbsp. oil, saute raw scallops for about 5 minutes. Cool 15 minutes. Combine remaining oil and the rest of ingredients. Add to scallops and marinate in the refrigerator 24 hours. Ready to eat.

*Note:* 1 lb. raw or cooked shrimp may be substituted for scallops. Omit sauteing if cooked shrimp are used.

## SCALLOP CASSEROLE

1 cup mushrooms, sauteed in butter. Add:
1 cup chopped green pepper or ½ green, ½ red. When soft add:
3 cups scallops, quarter if large ones.

Cover and simmer for 6 to 8 minutes. Meanwhile make 2 cups white sauce. In a small bowl mix 1 egg yolk, 1 ounce vermouth, dash Worcestershire sauce. Add to white sauce and stir into scallops. Put in casserole, cover with Parmesan cheese. Place under broiler until brown and bubbly. Add chopped parsley and serve.

## PICKLED MUSSELS

1 tsp. small red dried peppers
2 bay leaves
1 cup wine vinegar

1 cup water
2 cups cooked mussels

Combine pickling ingredients. Put mussels in mixture and let stand at least 3 days before eating. Store in refrigerator. Small steamed clams may be substituted.

# PIZZA A LA SEAFOOD

Use prepared pizza crust or make your own dough. Spread oil lightly on pan. Preheat oven to 400 degrees. Carefully spread dough in pan and pinch along the rim. Brush lightly with olive oil. Mix ¾ cup tomato sauce with ¼ cup tomato paste and spread on dough. Lay on cooked crab, goosenecked barnacles or any firm seafood of your choice. Next add sliced stuffed olives, black olives and parsley and cover with slices of Swiss cheese. Brush with olive oil. Bake about 25 minutes or until light brown in a hot oven.

# SEAFOOD CREPES

*Batter:*

3 eggs beaten slightly            ½ tsp. salt
1½ cups milk                      1¼ cups flour

Mix together until smooth and refrigerate for at least 1 hour before using.

*Filling:*

2 cups medium cream sauce. Heat thoroughly. Add 2 Tbsp. dry sherry or sauterne, ¼ cup grated Swiss cheese, 2 cups cooked or canned shellfish meat, 3 Tbsp. chopped onions. Keep warm on low heat or prepare in the top of double boiler to prevent scorching.

*To bake crepes:*

Brush 8 inch cast iron skillet with margarine or oil; heat over moderately high heat until just beginning to smoke. Pour 2 to 3 Tbsp. batter into pan and spread this with the back of a wooden spoon. When lightly brown, turn over for about ½ minute. Place on plate and cook next crepe. Place wax paper between each crepe. Add butter to pan before each frying. When the batter is gone, spoon ¼ cup filling into each crepe, fold and place in buttered pan seam side down. Spoon remaining filling over crepes and add another ¼ cup grated cheese over top. You may substitute sliced almonds for the cheese. Bake about 15 minutes at 425 degrees F. until hot and browned.

# SEAFOOD MOUSSE

2 envelopes gelatin
4 Tbsp. lemon juice
2 small onions, sliced
*Blend for 40 seconds*

*Add:*
1 cup mayonnaise
¼ tsp. paprika
1 tsp. dried parsley
1½ cups cooked, shelled shrimp
    or 1 cup crab

Blend until mixed and smooth. Put into oiled mold and chill for about 4 hours. Cover plate with lettuce and turn mousse out of mold on lettuce. Trim with olives, pickles, lemon slices and whole shrimp.

*Note:* ½ cup cooked octopus may be substituted for shrimp.

# FRIED OCTOPUS

Clean, skin and wash a young octopus. Season a large kettle of boiling water with salt, a few peppercorns, 3 slices of lemon, 6 or so sprays of parsley and 3 sprigs of thyme. Drop octopus slowly into boiling water so the tentacles will spread and boil rapidly for 5 to 10 minutes, depending on the size of the animal. Remove octopus from the water to drain and cool. Cut into 2 to 3 inch pieces, dip the pieces into beaten egg, dredge in flour and fry in hot deep fat (370 degrees) for 3 or 4 minutes or until they are golden brown. Drain on paper towels and sprinkle with salt and freshly ground pepper.

# HERB-STUFFED SQUID

4 squid
½ cup cottage cheese
½ cup cooked spinach
2 beaten eggs
1 Tbsp. grated Parmesan cheese

Garlic to taste
Chopped parsley
½ cup tomato vegetable juice
1 Tbsp. tomato paste
Onion and celery salt, pepper

Clean squid by rubbing briskly with coarse salt. Wash and skin body section. Remove the head, tentacles and internal organs including the pen. Set on paper towels to dry. Squeeze liquid from spinach and blend for a second. Place in bowl and add cottage cheese, eggs, garlic, Parmesan cheese and parsley. Stuff squids and sew shut with strings or use turkey fasteners. Heat tomato or vegetable juice with tomato paste and season with onion and celery salts. When liquid is simmering, add squid and cook slowly for about 1 hour or until tender.

# BAKED CLAMS

1 pint raw clams, ground
25 to 30 crackers, rolled fine
Salt and pepper to taste

1 pint of milk
3 or 4 eggs, well beaten
4 slices of lean bacon

Add milk to the clams and stir in the cracker crumbs until the mixture is thick enough to drop from a spoon. Add beaten eggs. Pour into 'a buttered baking dish. Lay strips of bacon across the top and bake in a moderate oven for 45 minutes or until firm. 4 to 7 servings.

# SEAFOOD FRITTERS

¾ cup cracker crumbs
2 beaten eggs
2 cups ground seafood (raw)
1 Tbsp. melted butter
Dash or two of fresh
   ground pepper

Dash of seafood seasoning
   or salt
½ cup milk or clam juice can
   be added to wet to desired
   consistency

Mix ingredients and form into small patties. Fry in fat that has been heated to about 375 degrees for about 2 minutes on each side.

Recipe can be used for ground clams, sea cucumbers, snails, mussels, limpets, octopus, abalone, chitons or cut-up oysters.

# BEEFY CLAMS IN A BLANKET

1 head of cabbage
2 cups cooked rice
1 pound hamburger
1 cup drained, ground clams
1 cup tomato juice or
   cabbage water
1 fresh tomato

1 medium onion, chopped
¼ tsp. thyme
1 tsp. dried parsley
½ tsp. celery salt
1 raw egg
Salt and pepper to taste

Cut core out of cabbage and cook in boiling salted water long enough to separate the leaves by pulling from the bottom. Avoid tearing the leaves if possible. Lay leaves on paper toweling to drain and cool. Brown chopped onion and stir in hamburger. Stir and cook until the meat is no longer pink. Add the other spices and clams. Set aside while you cook the rice. When all ingredients are cool enough to handle, stir the rice and egg into the meat mixture. Place about ½ cup mixture into each cabbage leaf. Fold over four ways and secure with a toothpick. Place folded side down on buttered baking dish. Use a small enough pan so sides are touching. Place a thin slice of tomato on top of each roll and pour liquid over the rolls before placing in a 350 degree oven. Cover for the first 10 minutes, then remove the cover and continue cooking for the next 30 minutes. Add a little more juice if liquid boils away.

## CLAM CHOWDER

4 to 6 medium potatoes, diced
1 medium onion, diced
4 strips bacon

1 cup minced raw clams (1 or 2 6½ oz. cans), amount depends upon how clammy you like it
2 large cans milk (13 oz.)
3 cups water

In a 4 quart pan, fry bacon until crisp. Drain and crumble; set aside. In about 3 Tbsp. bacon fat, saute onions and potatoes until both are lightly browned. Add raw clams and enough water to cover. Cook until potatoes are tender. When using canned clams, add them undrained after potatoes are cooked. Cool, add milk and about 3 cups water. Heat, but do not boil. Makes about eight 1 cup servings depending on the amount of potatoes and clams used.

## SHRIMP DIP

1 pkg. (8 oz.) cream cheese, softened
1 can cream of celery soup
2 tsp. lemon juice
¼ tsp garlic or onion salt (optional)

Dash of paprika
1 cup shrimp, diced (tiny shrimp may be used whole)
¼ cup mayonnaise

Combine all ingredients gradually into softened cream cheese. Add mayonnaise. Stir shrimp in last. If the consistency is too thick, add a little cream or canned milk. Try substituting cooked crab, ground clams or seafood of your choice. The thicker dip may be used as a spread for open-faced sandwiches. Trim with ripe and green olives.

# SHRIMP FRIED RICE

2 cups rice, cooked
1 cup onions, chopped
1 cup celery, sliced thin
½ green pepper, sliced
   (optional)
2 strips bacon

2 eggs, slightly beaten
2 Tbsp. soy sauce
1 cup shrimp, cooked
⅓ cup slivered almonds
4 green onions, chopped

In a skillet or wok, using moderate heat, fry bacon until crisp. Remove bacon, drain on paper toweling and crumble. Stir-fry onions and celery in the bacon drippings for 2 minutes. Add rice and stir-fry for 5 minutes. Reduce heat to low; add bacon bits and soy sauce. Add shrimp and heat for about 1 minute or more. Pour eggs over top of rice mixture. Stir-fry for about 2 minutes or until egg is just cooked. Serve with slivered almonds and chopped onions sprinkled on top. More soy sauce may be added at the table, if desired. Makes 3 to 4 servings.

# SHRIMP PATTIES

2 cups Alaska canned shrimp
2 eggs, beaten
6 crushed crackers
Dash of salt and celery salt
½ tsp. paprika

⅛ tsp. curry powder
½ tsp. lemon peel or substitute
¾ tsp. commercial seafood
   seasoning salt

Mix thoroughly, form into patties and fry on both sides in margarine. Serve on warm sesame seed buns spread with margarine or butter and mayonnaise.

To use large shrimp, such as Hood Canal shrimp, grind shrimp coarsely; add another egg and 1 tsp. lemon juice to recipe above.

Serve with pickles, relish, lettuce or sprouts. Makes 4 or 5 patties.

# SHRIMP WIGGLE

This recipe has been a favorite in our house for over twenty years. For a casserole-type dish made in a single pan on top of the stove, this one will not only save time, but will certainly please the diners.

Melt 4 tablespoons butter. Stir in and blend 2 tablespoons flour. Gradually add 1¼ cups milk. Add 1 cup shrimp (drained), 1 cup drained peas and ¾ cup of combined chopped olives, celery and parsley. Add paprika and celery salt. Lower heat and stir in 1 egg yolk. Stir and thicken. Add 1 tsp. lemon juice and salt. Serve on toast or rice. Serves about 3. The pan may be put into a medium oven to keep warm until ready to serve.

# SHRIMP KEBABS

24 large shrimp or scampi
2 medium size zucchini
16 or so mushroom caps

*Marinade:*

| | |
|---|---|
| 1 clove of crushed garlic | ½ cup lemon juice |
| 1 bay leaf, crushed | ½ cup olive oil or a good |
| ½ tsp. salt and pepper | cooking oil |

Simmer raw shrimp about 3 minutes. Cool quickly and remove shells. Slice the zucchini thin and wash the mushrooms. Place all the ingredients into bowl. Mix the marinade and pour over ingredients. Let stand for an hour or more. When ready to cook, drain but save the marinade. Arrange the shrimp, caps, and zucchini alternately on metal skewers, or, if you are using the small shrimp, you can use the wooden skewers. Wrap two to a foil package and place on a greased pan with the folded side up. Cook in hot oven (425 degrees F.) for about 15 minutes. Open foil, brush with remaining marinade and cook another 10 minutes.

Serve with lemon slices, tossed salad and hot rolls.

# JAMBALAYA

2 cups water
1 tsp. salt
1 cup rice

Cook rice until tender and water is absorbed, about 20 minutes. Keep covered and set aside.

2 lbs. raw shrimp, peeled and deveined
6 Tbsp. butter
1½ cups finely chopped onion
1¾ cups (1 lb. can) tomatoes, drained and chopped, save liquid
1 small can tomato paste
½ cup finely chopped celery
1 Tbsp. finely chopped parsley
¼ cup finely chopped green pepper (optional)
2 Tbsp. finely chopped garlic (optional)
¼ tsp. ground cloves
¼ tsp. black pepper
½ tsp. cayenne pepper
½ tsp. dried thyme
1 lb. ham, cut into ½ inch cubes

In a heavy kettle, saute onions in butter until soft and golden. Add tomatoes, tomato liquid and tomato paste. Then add celery, parsley, seasonings, plus 1 tsp. salt. Cook over moderate heat, stirring frequently until vegetables are soft. Add shrimp and ham and cook 5 minutes more. Add rice, stirring mixture over moderate heat until any liquid has been absorbed. Serves 6 to 8.

*Note:* Less than a pound of leftover ham has been used. Everything can be prepared up to the point of adding shrimp several hours in advance, or the day before serving. Reheating improves flavors, but be careful of overcooking the shrimp.

# COOKING AND CLEANING CRABS

Two methods are used for cooking and cleaning crabs. One is to simply drop live animal into boiling salted water for 12 to 15 minutes.

The other highly recommended method is to kill and clean the crab BEFORE it is cooked. Crabs cooked this way save space in the cooking pot, cut down on cooking odors, make subsequent cleaning less messy, have better flavored meat, and keep longer under refrigeration due to better penetration of salt. For the next six easy steps, you will need rubber gloves, a sharp heavy knife and a mallet or hammer:

1. With gloves, grasp the live crab from the rear, holding one or two legs firmly. Turn the crab on its back on a cutting board.

2. Position a sharp, heavy knife in the center of the crab between the legs, then hit sharply with the back of the knife to kill the crab.

3. Pry off the back and break in two by folding up and and then down.

4. Shake out viscera from each half and pull out gill filaments.

5. The claws and legs may be twisted off and cracked before cooking, if so desired. Wash all parts well before dropping into boiling water.

6. Add 3 to 5 ounces of salt per gallon of fresh water, bring to boil, add crab parts, and boil 15 minutes after the water returns to boiling. After removing crabs from water, immediately chill with ice or cold water.

To clean the legs, the secret is to crack, not crush the shells before shaking out the meat. First, start at the tip section and grasping the large section with one hand, pull out and up with the other hand to remove the cartilage filament. Lay leg on edge and rap sharply against the side of bowl to shake out the piece of meat whole. Repeat the process for remaining section and with all the legs.

# CRAB SOUFFLE

2 cups flaked, cooked crabmeat
¾ cup milk
2 slices of medium sized onion
A few sprigs of parsley
3 Tbsp. butter
3 Tbsp. flour

2 eggs, yolks and whites
  separated and each beaten stiff
1 Tbsp. lemon juice
½ tsp. salt and ¼ tsp. pepper
  or season to taste
½ cup buttered crumbs

Scald the milk with parsley and onion. Remove parsley and onion. Melt butter, stir in flour; when smooth, gradually add the scalded milk. Stir in beaten egg yolks after sauce thickens, take from fire and fold in stiffly beaten egg whites. Butter a mold, arrange a layer of crab, season with a few drops of lemon juice, salt and pepper, then a layer of sauce and so on until materials are used up. Cover top with buttered crumbs. Set mold in a pan of hot water and bake at 350 degrees until firm (about 30 to 45 minutes). 4 servings.

# A VERSION OF NORA BERG'S CASSEROLE

Layer cooked egg noodles with flaked crab meat, drained peas and some hard-boiled eggs. Over this pour condensed mushroom soup to which you have added celery, green peppers and dash of Tabasco. Cover with bread crumbs. Dot with butter. Bake 30 minutes at moderate heat.

Nora Berg is to be remembered for her colorful life as a beachcomber in the Copalis Beach area of Washington State. If you want to be a beachcomber, use beach peas instead of canned peas.

# HOW TO DRY SEAWEED

Seaweed can easily be dried in a barely warm oven, in a dehydrator, or by hanging it on a clothes line on a warm sunny day. First wash it carefully and thoroughly in fresh water being careful to remove any encrustations and eggs that may have been deposited by small marine animals. After the seaweed is thoroughly dried, store in air tight containers in a dry place. To use as fresh seaweed, reconstitute by placing dried pieces in fresh water a few minutes. Do not let it stay in water for a long period of time.

# SEAWEED CHIPS
*(Deep fat fried seaweed)*

Drop fresh Sugar Wrack seaweed that has been washed and patted dry, into hot fat for just 1 second. For ease of handling use tongs. Remove and immediately sprinkle with either sesame seeds or sugar.


# PIGS IN SEAWEED

Wash freshly gathered seaweed, either *(Gigartina spp.)* or *(Laminaria spp.)*, several times in fresh water. Cut in strips about 4 inches long by 2½ inches wide. Wrap the strips of seaweed around "Brown and Serve" sausages. Fasten the seaweed securely with toothpicks. Bake in a 350 degree oven for 15 to 20 minutes. The seaweed should be brown and crispy on the outside. Raw pork link sausages may be substituted, but precook them 10 minutes and drain off excess fat before wrapping the sausages in the seaweed.


# SEAWEED MARINADE

Wash freshly gathered seaweed in cold water. Then place in colander and pour boiling water over the seaweed. Drain and place in marinade several hours before serving.

*Marinade:*

| | |
|---|---|
| ¼ cup vinegar | 1 Tbsp. sugar |
| 1 tsp. soy sauce | ⅓ tsp. salt |


# STUFFED SEAWEED FRONDS

*Combine:*

| | |
|---|---|
| 2 cups cooked rice | 1 medium onion, chopped |
| ¼ lb. raw ground beef | 1 tsp. soy sauce |
| ¼ lb. chopped mushrooms | |

Drop dried seaweed fronds into boiling water for about 1 minute, spread carefully. On each frond place 1 Tbsp. of stuffing, then roll and place in steamer. Stack the rolls neatly in a steamer; pour 2 cups boiling water over all, then set it on the stove and steam slowly for 50 minutes.

# KELP SWEET PICKLES

Collect fresh Bull kelp *(Nereocystis luetkeana)* early in the summer, if possible. Select stipes (stems) that are about 8 to 10 feet long. Cut off the bulb end and the narrow end (smaller than 1 inch across), and dispose of the trimmings in your compost or garden. Keep about 12 to 14 feet of stems that are of nearly uniform size.

Peel stems and rinse in cold water. Cut into slices about ¾ inch wide. Cover with boiling water and allow to stand until the next morning. Weight down with a heavy plate to keep pickles under the water. For the next two mornings, drain off water and cover with fresh boiling water. On the fourth morning drain and cover with a boiling mixture of 8 cups sugar, 2 Tbsp. non-iodized salt, 4 drops green food coloring (optional), and 4 cups white vinegar. Drain, reheat, and pour boiling vinegar mixture over kelp for two mornings. On the 7th day you are ready to seal. Fill hot jars with kelp and hot syrup, put on lids and place in 5 minute hot water bath to insure the lids are sealed.

# SWEET PICKLE RELISH

To make your own sweet pickle relish for tartar sauce, take a cup of kelp pickles (drained), 1 small onion and a few red pepper seeds and put into a blender. Grind until it is the right consistency or put through a food grinder using the fine attachment. Put in jar and add enough vinegar to thoroughly moisten, about ¼ cup. Set in refrigerator for 24 hours. Use only glass jars to store foods that contain vinegar or lemon.

# TURKISH TOWEL PUDDING

½ cup loosely packed Turkish          Pinch of salt
  *(Gigartina spp.)* seaweed          1 tsp. vanilla
3 cups milk                           ½ cup sugar

Cook seaweed, milk and salt in a double boiler for 30 minutes. Remove from heat and strain through a cheesecloth, gently pressing the mixture through the cloth. Add sugar and vanilla, mix well. Pour into individual dessert dishes or a mold. Let set several hours or until the next day. Serve with sliced bananas, or fresh berries, and whipped cream.

*Variations:*
1. Add a beaten egg 2 minutes before removing from heat.
2. After mixture is strained, add ½ cup chocolate chips. Beat with egg beater until dissolved.

# TURKISH TOWEL COUGH SYRUP

½ cup tightly packed Turkish          2 cups water
  Towel *(Gigartina spp.)*            1 lemon
  seaweed (dried seaweed,             2 Tbsp. honey
  reconstituted, may also
  be used)

Cook seaweed and water in a double boiler for 30 minutes. Strain. Add lemon and honey and mix well. The mixture will keep in the refrigerator for 5 days. Try taking 2 Tbsp. for cough.

# TURKISH TOWEL HAND LOTION

Cook any amount of Turkish Towel seaweed with water – 1 part seaweed to 4 parts water – in a double boiler stirring occasionally for about 20 minutes. Remove from heat and strain. If you wish, add one or two drops of your favorite fragrance. If you store in the refrigerator, it will keep about a week. Make a small amount at a time.

# INDEX

# GLOSSARY

**Alga** — any plant of a group *(Algae)* comprising practically all seaweeds. Represented in this book *(Chlorophyceae)* green, *(Phaeophyceae)* brown, and *(Rhodophyceae)* red to black.

**Antennae** — feelers on the head of shrimp, crab, and lobster.

**Bivalve** — shellfish having two shells hinged together by a muscle.

**Caliber** — instrument used for measuring the distance across the back of a crab or an abalone.

**Cannibalistic** — devours its own kind.

**Carapace** — hard shell covering body on crabs, shrimp and lobster.

**Carnivorous** — prying or feeding on animals.

**Frond** — leaf-like part of seaweed.

**Holdfast** — secures seaweed to hard surfaces.

**Intertidal** — area between high tide mark and low tide mark.

**Kelp** — brown seaweed.

**Jig** — fishing lure used for dropping to the bottom and jerking line up rapidly.

**Operculum** — a protective trap door used for closing the shell.

**Radula** — a rasp-like tongue used for boring holes or scraping food from rocks.

**Spat** — a juvenile or young oyster which appears on the shells of mature oysters, rocks, etc.

**Stipe** — stem-like part of most seaweeds.

**Substratum** — the substance or base on which an organism grows.

**Tube feet** — special organs for collecting food or for movement.

**Valve** — one of two parts of a clam shell or one of the plates covering a barnacle.

# ADDITIONAL NOTES

## TIPS ON ALTERNATE WAYS TO OPEN OYSTERS

### Hot Water Bath

This method slightly firms the oyster, but is easier for those who have a difficult time opening oysters the traditional way with an oyster knife. Unless you are buying the oysters in a shell, it may be illegal where you live to do this. Returning the empty shells to the beach at the tide level in which you found them assures us that the crop will propagate itself. Check your local Fish and Wildlife regulations.

Drop live oysters in boiling water for about two minutes. Remove from the boiling water with tongs and place on flat surface. Force open the shell with a gloved hand and use the oyster knife to cut the muscle. Most of the shells with be partly open. Remove from the shell and cool immediately to stop the cooking process. For those who are unable to return the shell to the beach, select only those oysters that are free of spat.

### Microwave Method

Place the heavy side of the oyster down in a heavy, deep paper plate or similar dish. Cover completely with paper towel. Microwave polyethylene wrap may be used for a cover, however the rough edges may puncture holes in it. Place oysters in the microwave oven on high heat for a minute or so depending on the size of the oysters and how many you do at one time. The shells will not be popped clear open, but there should be space to insert the oyster knife in to cut the muscle.

Caution: Some oysters may pop in the oven scattering fragments of shells in your oven.

Algae, (common name, seaweed), are a group of marine plants that provide their own food by means of photosynthesis and in turn provide food for a multitude of marine animals. These marine herbivores consume the algae and they in turn become food for the carnivores in the saltwater. Since all fresh water from our land masses eventually makes its way to the sea, this water carries along with it valuable minerals that are absorbed by marine algae.

Basically algae is broken into four Phyla or divisions which does not include the microscopic ones. The first is the *Cyanophta* or Blue-Green. An example of this group would be *Spirulina* which has been used for dieting and other purposes. *Chlorophyta* or Green algae is usually found at high tide levels on the beach. An example is the *Ulva* found on page 46. At medium or low tide levels you will probably find *Phaeophyta* or the Brown algae which includes the various kelp (p. 47 and Sugar Wrack on opposite page.) *Rhodophyta* or Red algae may only be found growing at low tide levels. The Turkish Towel on page 49 is an example, however some Red algae is almost black in color.

Carrageenia is one of the hydrocolloids produced by red algae which can act as an emulsifier, stabilizer and viscosifier (adhesive) when used in food products, medicines, industrial products, textiles, and others. Alginic acid is found in all the larger Brown seaweeds as well as some of the smaller. Arrange a frond of seaweed on a piece of paper and it will produce its own glue. Because of limited space, only a few of a list of sixty-six products that may contain some by-product of seaweed are listed.

Sulfa suspension
Bulking laxatives
Surgical jellies
Dental impression compounds
Bakery goods and meringues
Candy and puddings
Dry ice cream mix
Paints
Gummed tape

Insulation board
Toothpaste
Aspirin compound
Tires
Foam cushions
Size compound
Paper bags
Cheese

# NOTES

# ADDITIONAL BOOKS
### by Authors
### Marjorie Furlong and Virginia Pill

*Starfish: Guides to Identification, Methods of Preserving*

*Wild Edible Fruits and Berries*

*Edible? Incredible Pondlife*

# OTHER RECOMMENDED BOOKS

*Oyster Cookery*

*The Pacific Northwest Salmon Cookbook*

*The Abalone Book*

*Sea Vegetables*

*Common Seashore Life of the Pacific N.W.*

*Our Underwater World*

*Seafood Cookery*

*Saltwater Fishing in Washington*

*Oregon Saltwater Fishing Guide*

*Washington State Fishing Guide*

*Smoking Salmon and Trout*

Order From:

Pill Enterprises
N. 22790 Hwy. 101
Shelton, WA 98584